Seasons
of the *Heart*

A compendium of poetry spanning the seasons of the year

and the seasons of the heart

Leila Lynne Leidtke

AuthorHouse™ LLC
1663 Liberty Drive
Bloomington, IN 47403
www.authorhouse.com
Phone: 1-800-839-8640

Published by AuthorHouse 08/20/2014

ISBN: 978-1-4817-2828-7 (sc)
978-1-4969-0356-3 (e)

Any people depicted in stock imagery provided by Thinkstock are models,
and such images are being used for illustrative purposes only.
Certain stock imagery © Thinkstock.

This book is printed on acid-free paper.

author HOUSE®

Dedication

For my husband, Byron

For my readers: May you grow in wonder throughout your lives as you explore your own seasons of the heart.

SPRING

TIME, THE MUSE

Time flows on in an endless current,
Rushing swiftly toward the sea.
Eddies and ripples in the changing torrent,
Make watermarks on eternity.

Silver minutes slip through my fingers
As the hours swim slowly by.
They disappear as I try to grasp them
Streaming silently away to die.

The steady flow of the rushing current
Speeds ahead, snaking through the plain,
Slicing swiftly the crust of ages,
And once gone, never comes again.

A Boy and a Girl

A boy and a girl
Walk slowly down the sidewalk
Hand in hand
Intensely aware of it
Intensely aware of each other
Very much in love.

A boy and a girl
Sit together on a bench
Talking,
Discussing life
Ardently, fervently
Happy together in their oneness of spirit.

A boy and a girl
Share a casual soda
Share each other
Wonder at the world around them
Wonder at the things people do
Wonder most of all about each other.

A boy and a girl
Kiss ecstatically under a street lamp
Wrapped securely
In the knowledge of their love.

Essence of Love

I can't help thinking how much more

        I love you now than I did before.

Fleeting questions that perplex your brow

        have more meaning to me now.

Are your eyes more thoughtful,

        your hands more sure?

Does your golden hair

        have a greater lure?

Is there greater kindness

        in the things you say?

Does your ruling heart

        hold a greater sway?

Are your arms more gentle

        than they were before?

I know not, only,

        I love you more.

Author's Note: I wrote this poem in celebration of my first love 40 years ago. However, it also applies to my husband, Byron. I found this poem as I was searching through my old files of writings and it means as much today as it did when I wrote it.

The Butterfly

In and out and all about

My mind wanders,

Like a butterfly at play,

It flits and flies around all day.

Never stopping at one flower,

It sniffs them all within an hour.

Airborne again, it flees the wind,

Never being caught or pinned.

Fast in flight, it fights the sky,

At last it spins away to die.

My butterfly.

My mind's eye.

INTRODUCTION TO LIFE

He rose from the grave on the third day.
He talked with Mary at the break of day.
Peter and John ran to meet him when they heard the news.
"He's alive, not dead!" That's what Mary said.

They found Him not in the empty tomb
For He joined his disciples in the upper room.
And great was their astonishment, great their fear
To see the Master suddenly appear.

And they beheld his hands and side
And knew that for men, He'd been crucified.
Amazement and joy overwhelmed them all
To see Him standing there strong and tall.

"Life evermore is yours today,
As ye believe on Me," they heard Him say.
This Easter message of victory
Has remained the same throughout history.

For the One who offered it is here today,
He's alive, not dead, so the scriptures say.
And so does everyone who encounters Christ,
For He is the way, the truth, and the life.

EASTER PROCLAMATION

The trumpet resounds through the still morning air
announcing the news...
He is risen!

The grave is empty, silent
The early sun's rays peek into the gloomy caverns of the tomb
Revealing nothing more than grave clothes shed.

In the garden, lilies open fragrant petals
shining with vibrant life.
Their beauty proclaims resurrection life
to enquiring hearts,
to seekers.
They look for the One
Who has shed the tomb's barren cocoon,
and risen to glorious resurrection life.

This poem was inspired by the trumpet shape of a lily. I imagined the lily as God's flower announcing "He is risen" as if a trumpet sounds.

CLEANSED AND SET FREE

There is a place of refuge, beneath the cleansing flow
Of Christ's blood shed upon the cross so many years ago.
It was shed for all believers, all who seek God's presence there,
And the refuge freely offered is for all to freely share.

He heals me and renews me
As beneath the cross I go.

Oh, the deep, deep joy I'm feeling that wells up within my heart,
The relief from sin and misery, His forgiveness does impart.
No ills may dare assail me, while I stand amidst the flow.
Satan's arrows cannot reach me. God protects me from the foe.

He heals me and renews me
As beneath the cross I go.

Oh, the freedom that I'm feeling as I take my refuge there.
Oh, the sweetness of His presence and the blessing of His care.
'Tis the wondrous love of Jesus at the cross for all to share.
'Tis my hope, my pledge to ever meet my Saviour there.

He heals me and renews me
As beneath the cross I go.

I penned this poem during a church service one Sunday to encourage a friend who was going through a difficult time with a divorce.

LOVE

Love is something you do.

Love is watching a child enjoy feeding the lorikeets at the zoo.

Love is having someone give you flowers.

Love is the joy you have giving someone else flowers.

Love is so big you have to give hugs.

Love is so strong it lasts over the years and over the miles.

Love is God.

I was inspired to write this after spending an afternoon at the zoo with my God children and sharing their delight at the birds perching on their hands and heads to get small treats.

DAYDREAMS

As I gaze across the back porch,

neighbor's children play in their sunny patch of grass.

A small spotted dog yaps in excitement,

dashing madly after a badly tossed red rubber ball.

The wind tosses the arms of the old scarred maple.

The petals of the last few roses drift softly down

to the rich green carpet below.

The world is peaceful and pleasant here in my backyard.

STILL POINT

There is a still point within me.

All goes on in a flurry of motion.

People come and go.

Events, seasons, all are constantly changing.

The familiar places and things that I think of

With fond memory are all getting older and so am I.

Yet there is a still point within me:

a resting place where I find refreshment and consolation

after the noisy confusion of a fast-paced day,

a harbor of peace to find shelter from the storms of life,

a place of quiet contentment which changes not.

Jesus is the still point of my turning world.

I took the picture of a sundial while enjoying a county fair and it reminded me of this poem.

Wedding Day

Love brings forth two followers

     who would be true to the call of his trumpet

That sounds loudly and joyously in the gates of the temple.

Man and woman

     they stand together

     heads bowed before God Almighty

United in a bond of faith,

     a pledge to keep,

     a duty to perform,

     a portion to share,

     in rain and sun alike.

Season upon season they go,

     looking always upon Him

     who would lead them in the path of righteousness

     holding steadfastly to each other's hand.

Many years ago I wrote *Wedding Day* for a couple of friends who were getting married. It was later read at our own wedding.

SUMMER

Perfume of Love

Sweet Fragrance, heavenly sight
Flowers waiting for me tonight
The one I love, a treasure trove
Of comfort, courage, strength untold.

Help me Father, to be bold
To say the loving words of old
Help me to walk each living day
To serve anew with feet of clay.

Help me to demonstrate my love
My arms spread wide to give a hug
Help me most of all to lose
Myself in You, that I may choose

To live, to serve, to pray, to care
To be the one who's always there
A helpmeet for the Father's use
To bless my husband and to lose

The selfish pride that chains me down
The sin of waiting far too long
To do the things that I must do
To be with him and walk with You.

My husband surprised me with flowers one day. Following this we had a disagreement. When I showed him *Perfume of Love* the next day it healed both of our hearts.

OJ

The taste of strawberry jam in the morning

on warm buttered toast,

The pungent odor of coffee,

and the fragrant tang of orange juice,

Wake my senses to the morning's revived sense of being.

Breakfast – renewed strength to meet the day's challenges.

Behold the Lord

Behold the Lord, O ye His blessed children.

His beauty is perfect.

His holiness is complete.

His ways are just and right, lacking nothing.

His thoughts are high and lofty.

Yet His heart is tender toward us.

And His ears are inclined to hear our cries.

His strong right arm supports us

in our day of trouble.

And His word guides us

when our thoughts are darkened.

The Lord only is our salvation.

His way is the way of peace,

In this present time,

And for all ages to come.

WORSHIP

The presence of God wraps around me.

I am cradled gently in the warmth of acceptance.

Love touches my heart softly and I bask in the warmth.

A radiant life that lights my heart within,

And sets my feet to dancing.

THE RIVER

Time, the mighty river,
       rushes onward to the sea
Sweeping all within its torrent,
       moving on, relentlessly.

Never ebbing, never slowing,
       on the muddy waters flow,
Filled with fragments of the daydreams,
       all the moments men may know.

Bobbing brightly in the water,
       like the sparkling drops of foam,
Are the minutes spent in caring,
       loving someone that they've known.

All together stream the moments
       toward the river's end, the sea.
Stretching out, they calmly beckon us
       toward eternity.

Dearly Beloved

Love is never what it seems

  each day filled with golden dreams.

Wonderment of lover's touch

  little words that mean so much.

Feeling helpless, feeling strong

  Bursting into mirthful song.

Knowing that you just can't lose

  Telling others all the news.

Beaming joy from ear to ear,

  Just to say, "I love you, Dear."

THE GIFT

The joy of knowing ourselves

Comes from the giving

That starts within our hearts.

The joy of living

is in giving

A smile, a touch,

A shared moment of experience remembered,

A word of comfort,

A prayer,

Are all loving thoughts

Embodied in the wisdom of

A day spent in loving.

The Shepherd

Be still and cease from striving, O my soul,

For the Lord thy God is with thee all the day.

Don't hesitate to follow His sweet call,

He goes ahead to straighten out the way.

The closer that I follow by His side,

The greater is my joy, the less my foolish pride.

From earthly burdens He provides release,

And shares with me His victory and His peace.

His gentle voice is all you'll ever need,

To comfort you in times of dark dismay.

His shepherd's arm will guide you through the night,

And lead you into bright and glorious day.

So come with me and heed the Shepherd's call,

His glorious sacrifice was made in love,

To wash away the sin and guilt of all,

Who follow Him to heavenly folds above.

I wrote another poem years ago in the hopes that our church music director would set it to music. He said that it didn't have the meter to make the music flow naturally. Then I wrote *The Shepherd* and gave it to him. It was never set to music but it reflected my feelings about life at the time.

Ode to Vicki

Vicki's gone;
Her soul walks on;
With Jesus at her side.

No more tears,
He gently wipes her eyes.
No more pain,
She leaps and runs,
And dances in the skies.

The victory's won.
Her job is done.
And she is home at last.
Her story's told;
Our hearts unfold,
With echoes of her past.

The joy she shares
With all who care,
Both here and up above,
She'll ever be
With company,
Enfolded in God's love.

And now we know,
She shares a part,
Of history's long span.
Her life, a bright and shining star,
In God's almighty hand.

This poem is dedicated to Vicki's daughter, Gwen, who walked by her side in this life.

In Spirit

Gentle dove,

Sweet messenger of peace,

You steal silently upon me,

Soothing my aching heart,

Lifting my soul upward,

Toward the Shepherd,

Who waits patiently for me

To make my comfortable bed

In the cradle of His arms.

SUNSHINE

Sunshine streams through my windows
Sparkling white light announcing day.
As I look at things in new light
I contemplate the tasks of day.

The daily challenge newly faced
is robed by courage from the light
The brightness leads me
The whiteness cheers me
The streams of light are ever bright.

Once again I rise to beauty
In the world of daytime cheer.
And again I meet the wonder
Of the lovely vista here.

Dark days seem far behind me
While I walk in bright new day.
And the freshness all around me
Newly fills my thoughts today.

Birdsong drifts through open window
As the birds sing out their praise.
Life is lovely, come and see it
In their song, they seem to say.

Each morning lights the snowfall,
Turning leaves or bright new day.
Each season shows its treasure
Newly washed in bright array.

As the beauty fills my soul now
I anticipate the day.
And I wonder how creation
Shown anew is mine today.

Just before this book went to press I was inspired to write *Sunshine*.

AUTUMN

Step to the Music

There is no accounting in love

Hesitant, she glances furtively across a room

To make some eye contact.

He looks at her, trying to read her signal

A slight smile, pretending not to notice.

Bravely, he comes to ask her to dance

Emboldened by her smile.

She nods and follows him onto the dance floor

They step in time to the music

Smiling openly now

Waiting for the slow dance to grasp each other closely.

And then a moment of ecstasy, when they touch and hold.

WEATHER REPORT

Raindrops

    falling

        on my face,

            Teardrops

                from God's

                    Heavenly face.

Snowflakes

    drifting

        past my eyes,

            Bits of

                heaven

                    from the skies.

Sunshine

    streaming through

        my hair

            Happiness,

                Love,

                    And One who cares.

ROSES IN NOVEMBER

Roses in November
Ere the snow does blow
Are nature's offering tender
And leave a rosy glow.

Roses in November
Blowing in the breeze
Are highlights of the fall time
Before the winter's freeze.

Roses in November
Amidst the falling leaves
Make thankful hearts remember
Exquisite thoughts of peace,
Of times with our beloved
Like photos in the mind,
And family and friends we love
As years pass by with time.

Roses in November
Remind me once again
That God's creation blossoms
To make us think of Him.

I was walking down our street on November 15, 2009 when I came upon a neighbor's house where roses were blooming all over their yard. I took this picture and was inspired to write the poem..

Storm Crossing

The wind moans and grumbles

like a wounded beast seeking shelter in the eaves of the house.

The trees sough with rain sodden limbs

making their protest in dark of night.

Splatters of rain and whistling wind

are all around me

as I cuddle in downy blankets

listening to the storm crossing.

There was a terrifically loud storm that woke me up recently (fall of 2012) and I got up and wrote *Storm Crossing* at 5 a.m.

God's Waiting Room

Wait upon God for the answers;

to heartbreak and loss and despair.

Remember His loving forgiveness,

and kindness to hear every prayer.

He waits for the helpless to seek Him;

in faith, for His grace from above.

He answers their prayers with great blessings,

and showers us all with His love.

Moving, In His Time

When the cloud is moving,
and the Lord calls you away;
When your whole world falls around you,
in that dark and fearsome day;

Know this, my brothers and sisters,
That God has heard your prayer.
That He's leading you, like eagles,
To soar through cloudy air.

O let your cares and troubles earthward go.
Drop the weights that cumber; release the thoughts that slow.

Yes, catch the tailwind blowing,
As you see your old things die.
Leap from the tattered nest,
And ride the windy sky.

Fly on the slipstream over the storm,
Above the melee and the noisy throng.
Until you see His purpose,
Until you grasp His choice,
His promise will sustain you,
And your guidance be His voice.

This was written 6/6/93 to encourage dear friends when they were moving during a difficult time of unemployment.

GIVING THANKS
A Hymn of Praise in Autumn

I am grateful for gorgeous painted leaves of various shades... golden greens, browns, oranges, purple hues, scarlet...nature's symphony of praise to the Maker.

I am grateful for songs that play in my heart reminding me of joy and hope in this life and the next.

I am grateful for the opportunity to give of self to friends that become family and family that become friends.

I am grateful for time to play with dogs, kids, and those who share a playful spirit.

I am grateful for cozy rooms, soft chairs and rest from the day's labors.

I am grateful for blessings that come from every direction...revealing the hand of God in my life.

GETTING READY FOR ADVENT

Christmas is coming,
    and we are getting thin;
Oh what bad shape the world is in.
Floods and famines, war and strife,
People are dying...just struggling for life.

Christmas is coming,
    and all around town,
Are bright decorations, and you hear the sound
Of bells that are ringing,
    gifts that are bringing,
Help and support to the hungry ones.
God's servants are working
    from dusk until dawn,
Preparing the presents
    for those who have none.

Christmas is coming,
    and we see everywhere,
The ragged children with nothing to share.
But I heard it myself,
    from a wise Christmas elf,
That this season of giving
    would bless those living beyond themselves.

And not just at Christmas,
    but each day as it comes,
They will walk in the joy
    of God's holy Son.

This poem is dedicated to Peter and Cass Twitchell and all who went to the rescue of Honduran people stranded by Hurricane Mitch in 1998. I was involved in helping with this relief effort.

DAILY THANKS

I'm thankful for the little things

That happen when the day begins,

The sunlight bathes the sky and trees,

The softness of the evening breeze,

The flowers blooming near and far,

The twinkling of the evening star,

The trilling of a bird that sings,

A friend who at the doorbell rings,

The loving kindness of a stranger,

And God's protecting us from danger.

All these things mean a lot

And bring some welcome food for thought,

As I consider as I pray

And thank the Lord for each new day.

A WARM DOG

A warm dog on my lap

Comfortable, he sighs and sleeps

Reassuring me that all is well.

Sharing the intimacy of touch

He hugs me with his whole body and

Lets me feel his love

Deeply within my being.

In tune with my rhythms,

In touch, in heart, in love

My obedient servant and adoring slave.

As you might suppose my yellow lab, Champion, takes every opportunity to climb into my lap. He weighs over 100 pounds.

WINTER

For many years I have written Christmas poems and sent them to family and friends. You will see them collected in this section.

WINTER ROMANCE

Like the cool white snow of winter
    Drifting softly round each tree,
Is the sweetness and refreshment
    Of my Saviour's love for me.

Like the blueness of the sky
    Stretching forth eternally
Is the trueness of His heart
    Which is always loving me.

Like the crystal water flowing
    Quickly through the icy ground,
So His thoughts toward me are going
    To the life with Him I've found.

Christmas Spirit

The Christmas spirit is much much more,

Than festive, bustling, crowded stores,

Than holly wreaths on every door,

Than candy canes or mistletoe,

Or shining trees with lights aglow,

Or powdery, gleaming drifts of snow

Or presents tied with satin bow.

There's a sort of magic in the air, I'm told.

It can't be purchased with silver or gold.

Yet somehow the feeling never gets old,

Of family gatherings full of mirth

Of wonder and joy and peace on earth,

That lightens our hearts

At the Christ child's birth.

THE LEGEND OF THE CHRISTMAS TREE

The legend of the Christmas tree began some years ago,
When Boniface, a Christian monk, described the evergreen.
The tree has three corners, but still is one tree.
Just as Father, Son and Holy Ghost are one in three.

Throughout the Middle Ages, the Feast of Adam and Eve
Was held December 24th, Oh yes, on Christmas Eve.
The people decorated the lovely pine and fir
With apples and twists of bread to recall the Garden of Eden.

One night, Martin Luther was coming back from church,
Saw starlight from branches, the icicles on a fir.
He cut that little tree down and placed it in his home,
Put candles on the branches, and called his children round.
He told them that Jesus, the light of the world,
was born on Christmas day unto a maiden girl.

The people in Europe began to trim their trees.
They hung pretty glass ornaments, and trinkets and treats.
They celebrated Jesus's birth with symbols that glowed
With hope and joy for all to share throughout the whole world.

You might see a star at the top of the tree,
Representing the star leading wise men three.
You might see an angel on one of the boughs.
Angels proclaimed Him from town to town.
The bright lights show Jesus as light of the world.
The bells ring-a-ling songs of joy to be heard.
And under the tree, the gifts signify
Jesus, God's gift to us – for now and always.

Christmas Glory

In the hush and silence of the starry night
As the moon gleams o'er the snow,
Our hearts are reminded of a tiny babe
       who was born so long ago.

The shepherds quaked in terror
At the bright and glorious light
Of angels who invited them
       to see the wondrous sight.

Three kings came to see the child
To worship Him, they said.
Gold and rare perfume they brought
       and they laid them on His bed.

The world was filled with angel's song
That echoed through the earth
To celebrate the One who brings
       to seeking hearts, new birth.

And so, this year at Christmas time
and all the whole year through
Let God's love and peace and joy
       Bring happiness to you.

A Christmas Song

Come and join the celebration of the birthday of the King.
As at Christmas we remember Him of whom the angels sing.

Hallelujah, hallelujah!
Bright and morning star of love.
Twas for us He condescended,
Left His glorious home above.

As the wise men gazed in wonder at the tiny sleeping babe,
Star shone brightly, angels hovered, cattle lowed and horses neighed.

Hallelujah, hallelujah!
He was born a helpless babe.
Come to give Himself a ransom,
Give Himself the world to save.

All around the lowly stable shines the heavenly golden light,
Of the star that lights the answer to the end of man's dark night.

Hallelujah, hallelujah!
Earth and heaven are joined at last.
Golden words of sage and prophet,
In His birth have come to pass.

Christmas Cheer

The wonder of the glistening star,

Was felt by folks both near and far.

And in a manger, meek and mild,

The Saviour slept, a humble child.

Three kings came to worship Him

And bring their gifts to Bethlehem.

As Christmas comes again this year,

God's love warms and gives us cheer.

THE ANGELS' SONG

Christmas comes but once a year,
And young and old rejoice,
To sing the old beloved hymns
With loud and eager voice.

In Bethlehem a babe was born
The earth and heavens rejoiced,
While shepherds bent their wondering ears
To hear angelic voice.

The wise men, long ago
Came from eastern lands.
They traveled far to follow star
With treasures in their hands.

Gold, frankincense and myrrh,
Were for the baby king.
But priceless was His gift to them,
Eternal song to sing.

And round about His manger
They, along with other folk
Heard the song the angels sang
Of peace and joy and hope.

And now as friends and kin draw near,
To celebrate Christ's birth,
May peace and joy, the angels' song
Be heard throughout the earth.

Christmas Wonder

The most wonderful time is Christmas time.
The frosty snow, the shining stars,
The melodies that wrap our hearts
With hymns of praise and songs of joy.

Delicious aromas assault our noses
And frosty nights tingle our toes.
Calls come in and cards from friends
Parcels and packages wrapped in bows.

We gather once again around the tree
Family, friends and loved ones there.
Gifts and bows, string and paper,
Oh what a glorious Christmas caper!

We watch with awe and glee
The rapt faces of each girl and boy
Gazing eagerly at the tree,
Opening gifts with wonder and joy.

And once again we remember Him
Whose birthday we celebrate each year.
He comes to every wondering heart,
His love to make the New Year start.

And as we dash along our merry way,
We understand His grace anew.
The babe who was born in Bethlehem
Our glorious Lord and dearest friend.

STARLIGHT

A Christmas song is in my heart,
A song to make the stars delight.

They shine so bright,
And split the night,
To show us the majestic sight,

Of one small babe
In manger straw,
Who came to give His life for all.

An offering of love
From the Father's heart,
His plan of blessings to impart.

To all of those who will receive
His gift to men - eternal life.

Starlight was written many years ago. I made my own art to send this Christmas card with the poem.

Treasure of the Star

The wonder of the star filled night

Was the silence of the blinding light.

Bethlehem's star

Beamed the news near and far

Of the birth of a son

To the world to come.

From ages past to this present day

The star still shines to light the way

To the presence of the lowly child,

A tiny baby, and yet a king,

The one of whom the angels sing.

To us He came that winter's day

And comes anew each time we pray

For peace and joy, life and love

Our gifts from Father God above.

The Dream

She slept in silence

      While the night sky twinkled above her.

Her mission fulfilled.

      Comfortable warmth surrounded her

      And the child sleeping alongside.

A new arrival from eternal realm;

      A king clothed in swaddling garb,

A miracle cradled in straw,

      Waiting to fulfill ancient promise to us all.

WINTER DREAM

Starry night, the moon is bright,

Silver beams enchant our sight.

The branches bare, crisp winter's air,

All is calm; peace rules the night.

Snowy mounds embrace the ground,

A winter's dream is ours tonight.

Birth of the Lamb
(Meditations on Isaiah 9:7)

The Lamb of God was born quietly, secretly,
    In a rocky cavern near the fields,
        Where flocks grazed under a starlit sky.

How quiet it must have been that night.
    His cry must have blended
        with the bleating and lowing
            Of cattle, sheep, donkeys who rested there.

A few shepherds gathered around a camp fire
    Suddenly heard voices from heaven
        Saying, "Glory to God,
           "For He is born
                Our Prince of Peace."

They sought eagerly that Christmas night,
    The promised One,
        wrapped in long bands of pure linen,
        laid in manger straw.
            Even as we seek Him now,
              Our Prince of Peace.

His still small voice
    still echoes in our hearts, saying,
        "Glory to God,
           "For His mercy endures forever,
            "And His government shall never end."
           Our Prince of Peace.

The Advent Season

The goodness of God reaches our hearts,

As the celebration of Christmas starts.

Little remembrances, cards and calls,

Visits with friends, and Santa Claus.

Carols are sung from door to door.

Invitations to parties galore.

Candles are lit and wicks are trimmed,

Along with trees from limb to limb.

As far flung families reunite

To celebrate the Christmas night

With one accord to seek the Lord

And rejoice in blessings upon us poured.

He touches our hearts with peace from above

And enfolds us with grace and the Father's love.

Christmas Star

The star is bright

and fills the night

divides the darkness

from the light

Its radiant beams

reflect our dreams

reveal our yearning for the sight

Of one small babe

in manger laid

Whose love is felt

by all tonight..

True Peace

Keep the Christ in your Christmas,
   Let Him come into your life.
How happy you'll be that you found Him,
   In a world of trouble and strife.

He's ever ready to save you,
   From a life of confusion and sin.
But He won't push himself upon you,
   You've got to invite Him in.

He stands at the door, ever knocking,
   And patiently waiting to find,
Your heart opened wide to receive Him,
   And His heavenly love so sublime.

So keep the Christ in your Christmas,
   And the joy of knowing the Lord,
Will surpass all earth's treasures and riches,
   In the glow of His princely reward.

This picture was taken in Salt Lake City in a building with life sized Biblical scenes.

The Babe of Bethlehem

O tiny babe in manger straw,
The hope of every age.
How blessed is thy coming now
In meekness and in grace.

The baby born in Bethlehem
Was born for all mankind.
His coming was a gift to us
Of the Father's love divine.

Those tiny hands of roseate snow
Could they have made the sun to glow,
And moved the stars through space and time,
And fashioned man with art sublime?

And yet at Christmas time
We sense the wonder of His birth.
A tiny child, yet heavenly king
Of those who dwell on earth.

To seeking hearts, His is the gift
Of peace from fear and strife.
And those who find Him come to know
The way, the truth, the life.

SPIRIT OF THE NEW YEAR

In this new year, may you be blessed,
With peace and love and happiness.
The future now, we cannot see,
As we await eternity.

When we leave this vale and our time is done,
Our victories won and our race is run,
When heartbreak and woes are gone at last,
When earthly things escape our grasp,
Our spirit leaves to carry on and enter into realms beyond.

The time spent here is gone so fast,
And only love will everlast.
Our friends and family and times with them,
Become our inheritance, now and then.
When we look back on days ago,
Memories sweet or filled with woe,
The treasures of those fading years,
Are hearts drawn close through smiles and tears.

Don't wait until your time has gone.
Don't put it off. Don't wait too long.
This time is yours to love and serve,
To be with those who need you so.
The lonely ones in loss and fear,
And others whom you hold so dear.

To reach a hand, to speak a word,
To laugh and live and play and give,
And be for them a faithful friend,
Who prays and loves until the end.
Your joys will grow, your heart expand,
As you love and bless your fellow man.

Last year (2011) I ran out of time to write a Christmas poem. I wrote *Spirit of the New Year* instead and sent it in January 2012.

In Closing

As I read through poems I've writ through the years

My heart fills with gladness, my eyes fill with tears.

At the memories they generate

Of happy times of yore and late.

And as I see with eyes renewed

The blessings in my way God strewed.

I thank Him more as days go by,

For faithful friends and family,

For those who shared the way with me.

And for the times I've searched and found

The gold of earth, the hearts profound

Of ones who loved and cared for me,

And helped me here Your grace to see.

Isaiah 58:14 says 'I will cause you to ride on the high hills of the earth.' Some time ago I realized that the high hills are the hearts of men and women. The only thing that we take from this life is the love of God and others. So let us make time to visit those we have missed. To kiss those that need to be kissed. And to hug and say a prayer and let them know that we do care.

LEILA LYNNE LEIDTKE

About the Author

Leila began writing poems in high school and has continued writing them throughout her life. For years, she wrote Christmas poems and sent them out as Christmas cards. Some of these poems are collected here. Leila is married with three grandchildren and she makes her home in Delaware, Ohio with their yellow labrador. Leila has recently published a children's book titled *If I Were President*. A preview is available at BooksbyLeila.com.

It is Leila's fond hope that some of the thoughts expressed herein will encourage and uplift you in some way.

IN APPRECIATION

Photographic Contributions

I appreciate all who have helped me by contributing beautiful pictures to this effort. This book could not have been completed without your help. I appreciate Helen Palmer for helping me with contributions and selection of pictures that capture the essence of the poetry.

Page 5	Helen Palmer
Page 19	Helen Palmer
Page 27	Helen Palmer
Page 33	Amy Leidtke
Page 37	Helen Palmer
Page 45	Helen Palmer
Page 49	Helen Palmer
Page 51	Helen Palmer
Page 53	Helen Palmer
Page 55	Helen Palmer
Page 61	Emma Dixon
Page 67	Jack Shultz, Intricate Imagery Photography
Page 73	Emma Dixon
Page 76	Helen Palmer
Page 77	Jim' O'Malley
Page 85	Helen Palmer
Page 91	Helen Palmer
Page 97	Helen Palmer
Page 115	Jim Liddle

Editorial Contributions

My heartfelt thanks goes to my cousin, Wendy Hutchison, for her excellent editing of the poems for this book. She left no stone unturned in helping with punctuation, word placement, suggestions for clarity and review of the poetry with her insights. Thank you so much for all of your work.